DEAR LILLIAN

A LETTER ABOUT THE END OF LIFE'S
JOURNEY AND THE BEGINNING OF ETERNITY

GENE EDWARDS

Destiny Image® Publishers, Inc.
P.O. Box 310
Shippensburg, PA 17257-0310

"Speaking to the Purposes of God for This Generation
and for the Generations to Come"

ISBN 0-7684-2159-4
(Previously published by Christian Books Publishing House
ISBN 0-940232-43-X)

For Worldwide Distribution
Printed in the U.S.A.

This book and all other Destiny Image, Revival Press, MercyPlace, Fresh Bread, Destiny Image Fiction, and Treasure House books are available at Christian bookstores and distributors worldwide.

For a U.S. bookstore nearest you, call **1-800-722-6774**.
For more information on foreign distributors, call **717-532-3040**.
Or reach us on the Internet:
www.destinyimage.com

LILLIAN

is my wife's mother. She is 90 years old, and she is making plans to meet her Lord. One of the things that concerns her has to do with questions her grandchildren might have at the time of her death. She decided, therefore, that she would have a talk with each of them! In preparing to do this, she asked Helen and me to give her any insight we might have on the death of Christians and on things about the hereafter. Lillian has been a close friend of mine for about 40 years now. Until my mother died, they, too, were good friends. The following letter is my contribution to Lillian's inquiry. I trust it will also be edifying to you.

Dear Lillian,

So you are planning to die soon (I trust you remember that *your* mother lived to be 98!) and have some questions about what to say to your grandchildren about your death. Well, let's talk about it. But let's not begin with the question: *What will happen to Lillian after she is dead?* Starting there is really the wrong place to begin. Instead, let's ask this question: *Where did Lillian begin?*

When did you, Lillian, have your true beginning? After that, we will move forward to your birth, your salvation, death, and glory!

To put it another way, to really understand your future, we need to make a trip into the past. I invite you, then, to go back in time to your *real beginning*.

You see, if we began this inquiry at the point of your death, we would actually be starting in the *middle* of the story.

Where did you have your true beginning? At the time of your birth? Surprisingly, no, much further back than that. Get ready for a surprise!

⚮——————⚮

Take my hand, Lillian, and let's find that moment of your real beginning. That was so long ago. In fact, we will have to return to a point in time that predates the creation of Adam *and* even predates the creation of this realm.

Did you exist back *before* creation? If you were but a body and soul, the answer would be no. You would be a temporal being, one who had a beginning and, of course, an end.

But you are not just a body and a soul (see 1 Thess. 5:23).

You are part spirit. This means part of you came from some place other than this *material* realm. The physical belongs to the physical world, the spirit belongs to the spiritual world. Your spirit had its beginning in the spiritual realm.

Are you mostly a body? Are you mostly a soul? Or is it possible that you are mostly a spiritual being? It is unquestionable,

Lillian, the most important part of you is your *spirit*.

It is difficult, is it not, to think of yourself as having begun somewhere besides a little town in central Texas.

Part of you did begin 90 years ago. That *is* when your *body* began. Your body is temporal, guaranteed *not* to last over one hundred years!

(By the way, that may be the most exciting part of dying. You received a body many years ago which today is worn out. That tired old broken-down machine is wanting to quit. One day you will be rid of it, forever!)

What of your soul? Your soul began when your body did, but your soul, unlike your body, has no end. By definition, your soul is *everlasting*.

Everlasting means to have a definite beginning but no end. The soul of Lillian, which began so many years ago in a little town in Texas, is going to go on and on, forever. You will soon give up your body, but you will continue on as an everlasting soul.

Things are definitely looking up. You will get rid of a worn-out body, and your soul will be set free.

But let's not stop there, because you are not *primarily* a body, neither are you *primarily* a soul. Nor is your true beginning in Texas. Of a certainty, your end is not in a cemetery.

❧————————————❧

Let us journey backward through time in search of your beginning. The best news of all awaits us somewhere back there.

We journey back to the creation of our world. But this is *not* far enough. We must now travel back to that place that is *before* creation.

We are on our way to a place that existed before angels. We are going back to a time so remote it even predates the existence of Heaven. What could possibly have existed *before* creation?

There is only *one* thing that existed *before* creation, and that is *God*.

Come, Lillian. We have arrived at our destination. We have come to a place where God is the everything! He is all that there is. There is nothing else except God. Before creation, He is the *All*.

Now, Lillian, if you will hold onto my hand, we will dare to step *into* God!

Dare we? Yes. The Scripture assures us again and again that we are *in* Him!

❧————————❧

As we move into the very being of our God, we find ourselves in a realm where all things are light, where there is no such thing as death, where there is nothing temporal. There is *nothing* created here. Everything is uncreated. Everything is eternal. Everything is God! We are in Life itself. Or should I say, "We are in Life Himself"? His Life goes on forever...in both directions. There never was when God was not. There never was when His Life was not.

We stand in the realm of billowing revelation, light beyond all light. In Him there is unhindered brightness. We stand engulfed in shafts of incandescent glory.

What are we doing here, in a place before creation, where God is all? And dare we say that you, Lillian, had your beginning *here?*

Hold on tightly now. We are about to find the answer to that question, for we are about to plunge into the very center of the being of God.

❧———————❧

Look around. Remember, this is *before* creation. What you see all around you is the very Life of God. We are surrounded by a

Life much higher than human life could ever be.

It is in this mysterious place, in this mysterious age, that God was making plans to create. One of the things that He decided to create was you, Lillian. He had already thought up the idea of giving you a body and a soul. But He had also made another decision. Long before your Lord ever began creating, He had decided He would one day take a portion of His very own Life—a part of His Life that you see surrounding you now—and place that Life …*His* Life…in *you*!

Understand, it was way back here when your God chose to put His *eternal* Life inside you. He made that decision here in this mysterious and distant age! He chose you before creation; He predestined that a portion of His being be placed *in* you.

Lillian, *this* is where you began. In Him. It was here, in Him, that your Lord marked off a portion of His being to one day be placed *in* you!

Do you know what that means? It means the main part of you (the most important part of you) never had a beginning! Dear Lillian, there is a part of you that always has been, is, and always shall be.

This is the place of your true origin!

Let me say that another way. It was way back here that God predestined you to become one of His children. Lillian, the only way you (or I) can be our parents' child is by having the life of our parents passed on to us. And so it came about, in the council of God, He marked off a portion of His being to someday become one with you.

I will create the heavens. Then, on yet another day, I will create the earth. On still another day, Lillian will be born. She is one whom I have chosen to be My own child. On a very special day, on the day of her redemption, I will take this particular portion of Myself and place it deep within Lillian. This portion of My being will be the central essence of Lillian. She will have within her traits of My nature and of My Life. She will express a uniqueness of My divinity that no one else will. Lillian will be unique among all My children. This portion of

My Life, which I have predestined to be in Lillian and to become part of Lillian, will continue on…forever…from everlasting to everlasting.

Would you like to see that very portion of His divine nature that He purposed to place in you?

❧———————❧

Do you see that pulsating, vibrating, glowing, shimmering element of God? Have you ever seen anything so beautiful, so flawless, so unutterably perfect? That is *you*, Lillian. That is the portion of God that He has—here in eternity past—marked off *in* Himself to be placed in you. You are looking at that portion of your Lord's divine nature that is destined to be placed in you and to become part of you and one with you.

When will this wonder occur? At the time of your conversion. At that time the very Spirit and Life of God will become one with your spirit.

Behold, the *real* Lillian!

In the eyes of God, you, Lillian, are an eternal being. You had a long, rich history living in the center of the very vortex of God Himself. A portion of you was in existence long before a little baby named Lillian was born. Later, at the time of your salvation, this very portion of the Lord's divine nature indwelt you. And became one with you.

Reach out and touch that element, Lillian. Never forget just how beautiful, how indescribably beautiful, how holy, how pure this element of God is. Nor will that change when it enters into you at the time of your conversion. The beauty, purity, holiness, and perfection of that portion of God in you has not altered, and will not alter, throughout all your life as a Christian. Nor will there be any change in His life on the day you die...or the day after. Never forget the purity, the perfection, and the glory you see here. And most of all, never forget that this portion of God—like all of God—can *never* die!

It is almost time for us to make our way back to space and time, to the physical creation, and to earth. Would it not be nice if we Christians spent more time back here in eternity past seeing how wonderful we are?

But just before we leave, there is something else here you should see.

You have now stood in that place, in God, where you existed *before* the foundation of the world. There is something else here that has to do with you. It is another event that took place before the foundation of the world.

Before we view this hallowed event, may I ask you some questions? Have you ever wondered why God chose you? What provoked Him to predestine you to receive

His eternal life? Why did He love Lillian *that* much? Frankly, I do not know why He chose you, but I have always cherished that scripture in the Old Testament that says, "*I love you…because I loved you*" (see Deut. 7:7-8). Perhaps the answer lies in those verses.

Have you ever doubted His love for you? Especially on a bad day when you were doing everything wrong? Our sinfulness can raise serious doubts in our minds about His love, can it not? Did you ever ask yourself, "What is God ever going to do with a believer as poor as I am?" Well, if you have done this, dear lady, you have wasted an awful lot of time worrying for nothing.

God chose you long before you were born. And long before you were born, He also took care of your sinful state. Can you grasp this? He took care of your sinful state before He created *anything*!

When did He do this? Well, that is what we are about to see. And remember, we are in a time *before* creation!

Take my hand again, Lillian; let us visit that place where He took care not only of sin, but death, too!

Do you see something up there ahead? Do you know what that is?

Come closer.

There!

That is the Lamb who was slain *before the foundation of the worlds* (see Rev. 13:8).

What can I say to you about this holy and sacred event, this incredible act of love...except to point out that a marvelous thing happened back here in the eternals that was to later take care of all your needs.

Come, Lillian, for now it is time to journey forward in time. We are about to come to that place and to that very day when you were born.

━━━❧━━━━━━━━❧━━━

Do you recognize the young woman? That is Ada, your mother. She has just been handed a very beautiful baby girl. She has just named the baby. Its name, of course, is Lillian.

You might say that this is the day your body and soul had their start. (Keep in mind that the body is guaranteed to last *no more* than a hundred years! The soul is guaranteed to go on forever.) Note the sparkling personality this newborn has. Yes, that is your soul shining its delightful personality out through your body. But keep looking, for there is more to see. Look deep inside that lovely little baby and you will see your spirit. Your very own personal, unique, human spirit.

Alas, Lillian, your spirit is dead! Let me explain.

What is a newborn baby doing with something dead inside it? Your human spirit is dead because of the tragedy of the fall of Adam. Your ancestor, Adam, passed on to you (and to me, and to all the sons and daughters of Adam) a human spirit. But he also passed on to us—woven right into our DNA—the nature of sin.

When Adam was created, his spirit was very much alive. But his spirit died in the presence of sin. Since then, everyone who has ever come into this world has arrived with a *stillborn* spirit. You and I, and all of us, make our entrance into this realm with something dead inside us.

Well, we do not want to stop on this sad note, do we? There is a much better day out there that awaits you. Do you know of what day I speak? I speak of the day you become a believer. That is the day your temporary body and your everlasting soul intersect with that wonderful *eternal* Life that

God marked off in Himself before the foundation of the world.

Your God is by nature *spirit*, and His Son Jesus Christ—after His resurrection from the dead—became a life-giving Spirit. This incredible Life of God (*including* that part of Him that was marked off for you and destined to become a part of you)…is life-giving. Right now Lillian has something dead in her that needs to have life given to it.

What would happen if Lillian's dead spirit came into contact with His life-giving Spirit? Let's find out!

❧————————❧

Do you recognize that building over there? It is the Fourth Street Baptist Church in Wichita Falls, Texas. Do you remember what happened to you one Sunday morning in this building? Let's go inside.

See the young girl sitting at the end of the pew? The one next to the window? She is 16 years old. You had forgotten how beautiful you were, had you not? Watch now, as that lovely young girl bows her head.

Quickly, look deep inside her.

Her human spirit is still dead—just as dead as it was on the day she was born. But now turn around. Let us see what is happening *in* God!

A door in the heavenlies is opening. Do you recognize the scene? There is that portion of God that was marked off before the foundation of creation. That holy thing, so pure, so perfect...a portion of the very nature of God...is about to come inside the young girl.

See! His Life is coming out of that heavenly door and is passing through your body and soul. His Life—His life-giving Spirit, His resurrecting *Life*—is heading straight toward your dead spirit!

Remember, you had your real beginning *in God*. Well, right now that very portion of God is about to become one with you, today.

What you are seeing is that mysterious event called "being born from above" (see Jn. 3:3,7 NRSV). Your spirit is inside your body and soul. His Life is about to touch

29

your spirit. That young girl, in mystery beyond mystery, is about to receive the Lord...inside her...forever. That portion coming out of God's nature contains all of God. (All of God is in every part of God.)

The greatest single event of your life is about to take place. Part of God, marked off in Him so long ago, just now touched your dead spirit!

See!

Incredible!

Your human spirit has been brought back to life by His Life! Part of you just rose from the dead! But that is not the end of this wonder. There is more. Keep looking at that young girl! Watch! His Life, His Spirit, is now becoming *one* with *her* spirit.

Your spirit has been made alive. Now your *resurrected* spirit is coming into *oneness* with the Life of God. From this moment, the two are inseparable. Your spirit and His Spirit have just become *one*.

We will leave this place now. But keep this in mind: There is a part of you that has been resurrected from the dead, and there is also a part of you that has come from out of God Himself. His eternal Spirit has never known death and will never know death, and that Spirit is one with *your* resurrected spirit.

Yes, a time will come when you will lay aside your body, but the most important part of you, your spirit—made one with

God's Life and God's Spirit—will never taste death.

One last thing before we depart.

If you will look very carefully inside that young girl, you will see a tiny seed deep within her spirit. That tiny seed constitutes one of the greatest mysteries and one of the greatest glories that will ever be revealed.

You will very definitely see that mysterious seed again! On a *very* special day.

But we will talk of that a little later. Right now, let us return to the present, and there let us consider the future.

❧————————☙

What will happen in that moment when you breathe your last breath?

Actually, when Death comes he will have very little he can claim. He cannot claim your human spirit, for it has been resurrected from the dead. (And is one with God!) *Nothing* dies *twice*. What else, then, can he claim? Death cannot claim God's Life in you, simply because God's Life cannot die. Death cannot claim your soul, for it is immortal *and* redeemed...redeemed by the blood of the Lord Jesus.

What is there for Death to claim? He can claim only that which you are probably very willing, at this point, to let him have. He *can* claim that temporary body of yours.

He doesn't get very much, does he?

Have you ever realized just exactly what you are bequeathing to Death? He gets a worn-out body and with it, sin, which dwells in the members of your body.

You leave to him nothing more than sin and all past remembrances of the fall. *That* is what Death gets. You might say that you, not Death, get the last laugh.

And even as you render up to him your body, at that very moment you receive the *hope of glory!*

I think, Lillian, you know what takes place after that.

To be absent from the body is to be present with the Lord (see 2 Cor. 5:8 NKJV).

Your soul and your spirit (with the Life of God in your spirit), at that moment, are set free.

Do you remember what we saw back there in Wichita Falls the morning you became a believer? God's Life passed from the spiritual realm and came into you, there to become one with you. At the moment of death, the scene reverses itself. You pass out of the physical realm, back through that door, and once again enter into that spiritual realm where you began! You will return to the spiritual realm from which you originally came.

I have a notion the first face you will see as you pass through that door and enter the realm of the heavenlies will be that of a Man. You know Him as your Lord and Savior.

You are going to meet a Man in the heavenlies. A physical, *visible* human being in a realm where everything else is invisible and spiritual. As the old song says, there really is *a man in the glory*.

How is that possible?

Your Lord has already received His glorified body—a body that can be seen with the human eye, yet a body that has all the properties of the spiritual realm. His physical body has become like unto His spirit. The body, the soul, and the spirit of your Lord are so much one that the physical and spiritual elements cannot be separated. Look well upon your Lord, Lillian...and know...in that moment you will be like Him!

Having laid aside a worn-out body, but with a spirit that is alive and "back home," you will be able to look upon the very face of God, in all His ultimate glory.

Exactly where does all this take place? Quite frankly, Lillian, I do not know the name of the place. The Lord once said to the dying thief, "Today you will be with Me in *paradise*" (Lk. 23:43b). Paul said, "To be absent from the body [is] to be present with the Lord" (2 Cor. 5:8 NKJV). Will you be in a place called paradise, which, I assume, is some glorious part of the heavenly realm? Or are paradise and Heaven one and the same? I do not know. I can only tell you this. You will be with Him. Nothing else matters.

How long will you have to wait until the Lord returns to earth with the vast host of the redeemed and with the elect angels? Not long at all—not long for you, not long for Paul, not long for Abraham—for you will be living in a realm where there is no such thing as time.

And what will it be like when the Lord and you (and an innumerable host of angels and redeemed) return to this planet?

Let us see.

❧————————❧

There will be at least one hundred million angels coming with you (see Rev. 5:11). Add to that all of the redeemed who have "gone on before." That should be quite a sight!

Imagine! You standing in the heavenlies with that vast host, waiting for the door
between our two realms to open!

Gabriel will blow his trumpet and the
Lord will give a shout that will split the
foundations of creation. With that, He will
descend (with the redeemed and the
angels in His train) to claim His own who
are still on earth.

As you near the earth, you will experi-
ence the other greatest moment you will
ever live. Do you recall seeing that little
seed hidden so deep within your spirit?
Well, that seed is going to burst forth from
out of the depths of your spirit! Do you
know what that little seed is? Why, it is the

"hope of glory"! That little seed is your new, transfigured *body*!

You are going to receive a body that is like unto His—wholly physical, yet completely spiritual. Think of it! You will have a body and a soul that have become like unto your spirit.

At last, Lillian, you will be complete.

In that moment, you will have received full salvation! You will be as flawless, perfect, pure, and whole in your body and soul as you are right now in your spirit. You will be a completed daughter of the Living God.

As you approach this planet, you will see some incredible things happening down here on earth. The redeemed ones here on earth are going to see their decaying, sin-filled bodies change in the twinkling of an eye. *Then* they are all coming up to meet you!

And, oh, what a meeting that will be!

That will be the most spectacular moment that has ever been or ever will be.

What then?

Lillian, I would like to tell you that I understand everything I am about to say, but I do not.

First of all there will come forth a new earth to replace this old one.

Then comes the most exciting part... and the most mysterious: All who are redeemed are going to become one.

It appears, at least to me, that in our gathering together and becoming one, we shall find that we have, all together, become a *girl*—one glorious, beautiful, betrothed girl!

Who is this beautiful, flawless, *young* woman?

She is the most beautiful woman who has ever lived. She will carry within her all the gifts of her Lord. She will combine all of the personal traits of the God who gave her His Life. All those portions of divine nature, which were placed in each one of the redeemed ones, will now join together and make one complete, glorious *counterpart* for the Lord.

Radiating out from the young woman, so pure and perfect, will flow forth the second greatest glory that will ever be known.

Who is this girl?

She is the bride of the Lord Jesus Christ. And *you* are a part of her! There you are...in her. A glorious girl...perfect, holy, pure, without spot or blemish.

What takes place next is beyond all understanding and all telling. This lovely girl, more beautiful than anything that all words or poetry could ever describe, will then become *one* with her Lord!

At that indescribable moment, you will return to that place where you began.

Lillian, we are all going back to where we came from! The Lord Jesus and this girl will become utterly one. Then He who is the All will become the All in All. You will find yourself once more in the very center and vortex of God.

And you will be one with Him forever more.

Hallelujah!

Love,

GENE

❧————————❧

P.S. Lillian, if you really do precede me, when you arrive please give everyone my greetings. And tell Mother I'll soon be there.

REFERENCES

Even though I walk through the valley of the shadow of death, I will fear no evil, for You are with me; Your rod and Your staff, they comfort me. ... Surely goodness and love will follow me all the days of my life, and I will dwell in the house of the Lord forever (Psalm 23:4,6).

But God will redeem my life from the grave; He will surely take me to Himself. Do not be overawed when a man grows rich, when the splendor of his house increases; for he will take nothing with him when he dies, his splendor will not descend with him (Psalm 49:15-17).

On this mountain the Lord Almighty will prepare a feast of rich food for all peoples, a banquet of aged wine—the best of meats and the finest of wines. On this mountain He will destroy the shroud that enfolds all peoples, the sheet that covers all nations; He will swallow up death forever. The Sovereign Lord will wipe away the tears from all faces; He will remove the disgrace of His people from all the earth. The Lord has spoken. In that day they will say, "Surely this is our God; we trusted in Him, and He saved us. This is the Lord, we trusted in Him; let us rejoice and be glad in His salvation" (Isaiah 25:6-9).

...the day of death [is] *better than the day of birth. It is better to go to a house of mourning than to go to a house of feasting, for death is the destiny of every man; the living should take this to heart* (Ecclesiastes 7:1-2).

Do not store up for yourselves treasures on earth, where moth and rust destroy, and where thieves break in and steal. But store up for yourselves treasures in heaven, where moth and rust do not destroy, and where thieves do not break in and steal. For where your treasure is, there your heart will be also (Matthew 6:19-21).

Therefore I tell you, do not worry about your life, what you will eat or drink; or about your body, what you will wear. Is not life more important than food, and the body more important than clothes? Look at the birds of the air; they do not sow or reap or store away in barns, and yet your heavenly Father feeds them. Are you not much more valuable than they? Who of you by worrying can add a single hour to his life? (Matthew 6:25-27)

Then the King will say to those on His right, "Come, you who are blessed by My Father; take your inheritance, the kingdom prepared for you since the creation of the world" (Matthew 25:34).

...you will see the Son of Man sitting at the right hand of the Mighty One and coming on the clouds of heaven (Matthew 26:64).

At that time men will see the Son of Man coming in clouds with great power and glory. And He will send His angels and gather His elect from the four winds, from the ends of the earth to the ends of the heavens (Mark 13:26-27).

After the Lord Jesus had spoken to them, He was taken up into heaven

and He sat at the right hand of God
(Mark 16:19).

...there [is] *more rejoicing in heaven
over one sinner who repents than over
ninety-nine righteous persons who do
not need to repent* (Luke 15:7; see
also entire 15th chapter).

*Then he said, "Jesus, remember me
when You come into Your kingdom."
Jesus answered him, "I tell you the
truth, today you will be with Me in
paradise"* (Luke 23:42-43).

*That everyone who believes in Him
may have eternal life. For God so*

loved the world that He gave His one and only Son, that whoever believes in Him shall not perish but have eternal life (John 3:15-16).

I tell you the truth, whoever hears My word and believes Him who sent Me has eternal life and will not be condemned; he has crossed over from death to life. I tell you the truth, a time is coming and has now come when the dead will hear the voice of the Son of God and those who hear will live. For as the Father has life in Himself, so He has granted the Son to have life in Himself. And He has given Him authority to judge because

He is the Son of Man. Do not be amazed at this, for a time is coming when all who are in their graves will hear His voice and come out... (John 5:24-29).

My sheep listen to My voice; I know them, and they follow Me. I give them eternal life, and they shall never perish; no one can snatch them out of My hand (John 10:27-28).

Jesus said to her, "I am the resurrection and the life. He who believes in Me will live, even though he dies; and whoever lives and believes in Me will never die. Do you believe this?" (John 11:25-26).

Do not let your hearts be troubled. Trust in God; trust also in Me. In My Father's house are many rooms; if it were not so, I would have told you. I am going there to prepare a place for you. And if I go and prepare a place for you, I will come back and take you to be with Me that you also may be where I am (John 14:1-3).

I will remain in the world no longer, but they are still in the world, and I am coming to You. Holy Father, protect them by the power of Your name— the name You gave Me—so that they may be one as We are one (John 17:11).

For if, by the trespass of the one man, death reigned through that one man, how much more will those who receive God's abundant provision of grace and of the gift of righteousness reign in life through the one man, Jesus Christ (Romans 5:17).

For the wages of sin is death, but the gift of God is eternal life in Christ Jesus our Lord (Romans 6:23).

If only for this life we have hope in Christ, we are to be pitied more than all men. But Christ has indeed been raised from the dead, the firstfruits of those who have fallen asleep. For since death came through a man, the resurrection of the dead comes also through a man. For as in Adam all die, so in Christ all will be made alive. But each in his own turn: Christ, the firstfruits; then, when He comes, those who belong to Him. Then the end will come, when He hands over the kingdom to God the Father after He has destroyed all dominion, authority and power. For He must reign until He has put all His enemies under His feet. The last enemy to be destroyed is death. For He "has put everything under His feet." Now when it says that "everything" has been put under Him, it is clear that this does not include God Himself, who put every-thing under Christ. When He has done this, then the Son Himself will be made subject to Him who put every-thing under Him, so that God may be all in all (1 Corinthians 15:19-28).

But someone may ask, "How are the dead raised? With what kind of body will they come?" How foolish! What you sow does not come to life unless it dies. When you sow, you do not plant the body that will be, but just a seed, perhaps of wheat or of something else. But God gives it a body as He has determined, and to each kind of seed He gives its own body. All flesh is not the same: Men have one kind of flesh, animals have another, birds another and fish another. There are also heavenly bodies and there are earthly bodies; but the splendor of the heavenly bodies is one kind, and the splendor of the earthly bodies is another. The sun has one kind of splendor, the moon another and the stars another; and star differs from star in splendor. So will it be with the resurrection of the dead. The body that is sown is perishable, it is raised imperishable; it is sown in dishonor, it is raised in glory; it is sown in weakness, it is raised in power; it is sown a natural body, it is raised a spiritual body. If there is a natural body, there is also a spiritual body. So it is written: "The first man Adam became a living being"; the last Adam, a life-giving spirit. The spiritual did not come first, but the natural, and after that the spiritual. The first man was of the dust of the earth, the second man from heaven. As was the earthly man, so are those who are of the earth; and as is the man from heaven, so also are those who are of heaven. And just as we have borne the likeness of the earthly man, so shall we bear the likeness of the man from heaven. I declare to you, brothers, that flesh and blood cannot inherit the kingdom of God, nor does the perishable inherit the imperishable. Listen, I tell you a mystery: We will not all sleep, but we will all be changed—in a flash, in the twinkling of an eye, at the last trumpet. For the trumpet will sound, the dead will be raised imperishable, and we will be changed. For the perishable must clothe itself with the imperishable, and the mortal with immortality. When the perishable has been clothed with the imperishable, and the mortal with immortality, then the saying that is written will come true: "Death has been swallowed up in victory." "Where, O death, is your victory? Where, O death, is your sting?" (1 Corinthians 15:35-55).

Now we know that if the earthly tent we live in is destroyed, we have a building from God, an eternal house in heaven, not built by human hands. Meanwhile we groan, longing to be clothed with our heavenly dwelling, because when we are clothed, we will not be found naked. For while we are in this tent, we groan and are burdened, because we do not wish to be unclothed but to be clothed with our heavenly dwelling, so that what is mortal may be swallowed up by life. Now it is God who has made us for this very purpose and has given us the Spirit as a deposit, guaranteeing what is to come. Therefore we are always confident and know that as long as we are at home in the body we are away from the Lord. We live by faith, not by sight. We are confident, I say, and would prefer to be away from the body and at home with the Lord (2 Corinthians 5:1-8).

Even as He selected us in Him before the foundation of the world, having marked us out for adoption through Jesus Christ (Ephesians 1:4-5 Wuest).

And be found in Him, not having a righteousness of my own that comes from the law, but that which is through faith in Christ—the righteousness that comes from God and is by faith. I want to know Christ and the power of His resurrection and the fellowship of sharing in His sufferings, becoming like Him in His death, and so, somehow, to attain to the resurrection from the dead (Philippians 3:9-11).

But our citizenship is in heaven. And we eagerly await a Savior from there, the Lord Jesus Christ, who, by the power that enables Him to bring everything under His control, will transform our lowly bodies so that they will be like His glorious body (Philippians 3:20-21).

For you died, and your life is now hidden with Christ in God. When Christ, who is your life, appears, then you also will appear with Him in glory (Colossians 3:3-4).

Brothers, we do not want you to be ignorant about those who fall asleep, or to grieve like the rest of men, who have no hope. We believe that Jesus died and rose again and so we believe that God will bring with Jesus those who have fallen asleep in Him. According to the Lord's own word, we tell you that we who are still alive, who are left till the coming of the Lord, will certainly not precede those who have fallen asleep. For the Lord Himself will come down from heaven, with a loud command, with the voice of the archangel and with the trumpet call of God, and the dead in Christ will rise first. After that, we who are still alive and are left will be caught up together with them in the clouds to meet the Lord in the air. And so we will be with the Lord forever. Therefore encourage each other with these words (1 Thessalonians 4:13-18).

The Lord will rescue me from every evil attack and will bring me safely to

His heavenly kingdom. To Him be glory for ever and ever. Amen (2 Timothy 4:18).

In bringing many sons to glory, it was fitting that God, for whom and through whom everything exists, should make the author of their salvation perfect through suffering. Both the one who makes men holy and those who are made holy are of the same family. So Jesus is not ashamed to call them brothers. He says, "I will declare Your name to My brothers; in the presence of the congregation I will sing Your praises." And again, "I will put My trust in Him." And again He says, "Here am I, and the children God has given Me." Since the children have flesh and blood, He too shared in their humanity so that by His death He might destroy him who holds the power of death—that is, the devil— and free those who all their lives were held in slavery by their fear of death. For surely it is not angels He helps, but Abraham's descendants. For this reason He had to be made like His brothers in every way, in order that He might become a merciful and faithful high priest in service to God, and that He might make atonement for the sins of the people. Because He Himself suffered when He was tempted, He is able to help those who are being tempted (Hebrews 2:10-18).

Now we who have believed enter that rest, just as God has said, "So I declared on oath in My anger, 'They shall never enter My rest.' " And yet His work has been finished since the creation of the world (Hebrews 4:3).

…Their sins and lawless acts I will remember no more (Hebrews 10:17).

These were all commended for their faith, yet none of them received what had been promised. God had planned something better for us so that only together with us would they be made perfect (Hebrews 11:39-40).

But you have come to Mount Zion, to the heavenly Jerusalem, the city of the living God. You have come to thousands upon thousands of angels in joyful assembly, to the church of the firstborn, whose names are written in heaven. You have come to God, the judge of all men, to the spirits of righteous men made perfect (Hebrews 12:22-23).

He was chosen before the creation of the world, but was revealed in these last times for your sake (1 Peter 1:20).

But in keeping with His promise we are looking forward to a new heaven and a new earth, the home of righteousness (2 Peter 3:13).

And this is the testimony: God has given us eternal life, and this life is in His Son. He who has the Son has life; he who does not have the Son of God does not have life (1 John 5:11-12).

…written in the book of life belonging to the Lamb that was slain from the

creation of the world (Revelation 13:8).

Let us rejoice and be glad and give Him glory! For the wedding of the Lamb has come, and His bride has made herself ready (Revelation 19:7).

Then I saw a new heaven and a new earth, for the first heaven and the first earth had passed away, and there was no longer any sea. I saw the Holy City, the new Jerusalem, coming down out of heaven from God, prepared as a bride beautifully dressed for her husband. And I heard a loud voice from the throne saying, "Now the dwelling of God is with men, and He will live with them. They will be His people, and God Himself will be with them and be their God. He will wipe every tear from their eyes. There will be no more death or mourning or crying or pain, for the old order of things has passed away." He who was seated on the throne said, "I am making everything new!" Then He said, "Write this down, for these words are trustworthy and true" (Revelation 21:1-5).

The Ship

I am standing upon the seashore
and see a nearby ship spread her
white sails to the morning breeze
and start for the blue ocean.

She is an object of beauty and
strength. I watch her until at
length she is only a speck of white
cloud just where the sea and sky
meet and mingle. Then someone
at my side exclaims, "She's gone!"

Gone where? Gone from my
sight, that is all. She is just as
large in hull and mast and spar as

she was when she departed and just as able to bear her load of living freight to the place of her destination. Her diminished size is in me, not in her.

And just at the moment when someone cries, "She's gone," there are other eyes watching for her arrival, and other voices that take up the glad shout, "There she comes!"

And that is dying.

—Author Unknown

BOOKS BY GENE EDWARDS
A Tale of Three Kings
The Divine Romance
The Prisoner in the Third Cell

Introduction to the Deeper Christian Life
Living by the Highest Life
The Secret to the Christian Life
The Inward Journey

Letters to a Devastated Christian
Climb the Highest Mountain
Exquisite Agony
Overlooked Christianity
Rethinking Elders
Revolution: The Story of the Early Church
How to Meet in Homes
Beyond Radical

The First-Century Diaries
The Silas Diary
The Titus Diary
The Timothy Diary
The Priscilla Diary
The Gaius Diary

The Chronicles of the Door
The Beginning
The Escape
The Birth
The Triumph
The Return

To contact the author, write to:

Gene Edwards

P.O. Box 3450

Jacksonville, Fl 32206

Also by
Gene Edwards

100 DAYS IN THE SECRET PLACE

Gene Edwards, the master storyteller, has gathered together the writings of three Christian mystics from the 17th century: Michael Molinos, Madam Guyon, and Francois Fenelon. The writer of these "masters of the spiritual way" will be as lamp posts leading the weary traveler towards that secret place lovingly created by the Father.
ISBN 0-7684-2065-2

Additional copies of this book and other
book titles from DESTINY IMAGE are
available at your local bookstore.

For a complete list of our titles,
visit us at www.destinyimage.com
Send a request for a catalog to:

Destiny Image® Publishers, Inc.
P.O. Box 310
Shippensburg, PA 17257-0310

*"Speaking to the Purposes of God for This
Generation and for the Generations to Come"*